W9-CNL-280

J   474629
177   9.95
Gol
Goley
Learn the value of respect

DATE DUE			

LEARN THE VALUE OF

Respect

by Elaine P. Goley

Illustrated by Debbie Crocker

Rourke Enterprises, Inc.

Vero Beach, FL 32964

4391710

© 1989 Rourke Enterprises, Inc.

All rights reserved. No part of this book may be
reproduced or utilized in any form or by any
means, electronic or mechanical including
photocopying, recording or by any information
storage and retrieval system without permission in
writing from the publisher.

Library of Congress Cataloging-in-Publication Data

Goley, Elaine P., 1949–
    Learn the value of respect.

    Summary: Defines the concept of respect by
examples of how it may be shown in daily life, such as
demonstrating respect for another's wishes, religion,
or possessions, or respect for the beauties of nature.
    1. Respect—Juvenile literature. [1. Respect.]
I. Title. II. Title: Respect. BJ1533.R4G65 1988
179'.9—dc19   88-35315
ISBN 0-86592-387-6

Respect

474623

Do you know what **respect** is?

Respect is saying "Yes, Miss Brown" to your teacher and obeying when she asks you to water the plants.

You show **respect** when you play quietly if
your dad is reading the newspaper.

We **respect** our country and the Constitution of the United States by obeying its laws.

The people next door speak Spanish and have
piñatas at their birthday parties . . . they are our friends
and we **respect** their right to be different.

You show **respect** for your parents when you do what they ask . . . even if they're not watching.

You have **respect** for your safety when you
use the crosswalk.

If Jane doesn't want to skip rope with us, we won't insist, because we **respect** her right to be alone.

We show **respect** for our country by saluting
the flag and reciting the Pledge of Allegiance
every morning in school.

You're careful with your friend's toys because you **respect** the property of others.

We stand at the curb quietly and wait when
the school crossing guard tells us, because we
respect her and our own safety.

We show **respect** for wildlife when we
watch deer and rabbits from a distance
without disturbing them.

We put the dog in the backyard so that he won't run into the street and get hurt, because we **respect** his right to live a healthy, safe life.

When we are in church we are quiet to show
respect for God and his house . . . No matter what
religion we practice, we **respect** the religious
freedom of others.

We're careful with fires when we camp in
the woods because we have **respect** for nature
and don't want to start a forest fire.

In the summer we don't stay in the sun
too long because we need to **respect** its power;
it can burn our skin.

We feed the birds in the backyard because
we **respect** their beauty and their right to live.

Respect is loving yourself and others.
You are a special person who needs and **respects**
others just as they need and **respect** you.

Respect

It was Thanksgiving. The turkey smelled so good. Lisa and Lenny waited by the window for their aunt, uncle, and grandparents to arrive for dinner.

"Here they come!" shouted Lisa as she ran to the door.

Aunt Eve carried two pies. Uncle Ed had a bagful of chestnuts. Grandma handed Lisa and Lenny each a book.

"Thanks, Grandma," said Lenny, and he sat by the fire to read it.

Lisa frowned, took her book, and ran upstairs.

"I hate to read," said Lisa. "Why didn't Grandma bring me candy?"

Then Lisa got out her crayons. She began drawing all over the book as Lenny came into the room.

"Lisa, what are you doing?" said Lenny. "Books are our best friends."

Which child showed **respect** for books?
How do you show **respect** for property?

Respect

"Mmm, this is good," said Terry as he gulped down another piece of cake.

"Terry, it's time to go to the doctor for your checkup," said his mom. "We need to find out why you're so tired."

"Well, Terry," said Dr. Banks. "I know you'll feel better if you exercise more and eat less junk food. You need to lose some weight."

I'll eat goodies if I want to, thought Terry. As soon as he got home, Terry grabbed a handful of cookies from the jar.

"Terry!" said his mom. "No more goodies for a while. Don't you want to have more energy, so you can play ball with your friends?"

Terry stuffed a cookie into his mouth and ran outside crying.

What are some ways Terry could hurt his body by not showing **respect** for it?

How do you show **respect** for your body?